The BOX ROOM

ORCHARD BOOKS
96 Leonard Street, London EC2A 4XD
Orchard Books Australia
Unit 31/56 O'Riordan Street, Alexandria, NSW 2015
First published in Great Britain in 2001
ISBN 1 84121 793 X
Text © Sophie Hannah 2001
Illustrations © Helen Stephens 2001
A CIP catalogue record for this book
is available from the British Library
10 9 8 7 6 5 4 3 2 1
Printed in Great Britain

This book is to be returned on or before
the last d~ ~ ~ ~r~ ~ be~ ~~

The BOX ROOM

poems by SOPHIE HANNAH

pictures by HELEN STEPHENS

ORCHARD BOOKS

To Lauren Chappell
SH

To Nanan and Pop
HS

Contents

Our New House

My mum and dad both used to say
Our old house was a box,
So now we've moved, not far away,
To Thirty-two The Locks.

There's more room for our dressing gowns
And more room for our socks.
There's more room for our eiderdowns
At Thirty-two The Locks.

Our new house is right by the mill
On one side of the square.
Behind it is a big green hill
And trees are everywhere.

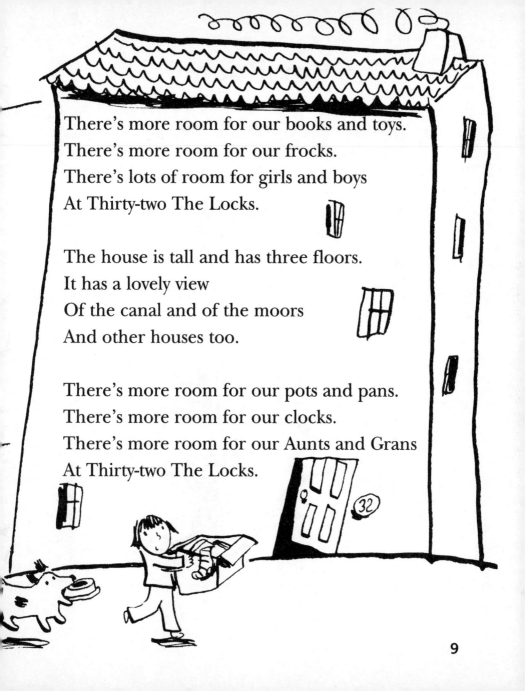

There's more room for our books and toys.
There's more room for our frocks.
There's lots of room for girls and boys
At Thirty-two The Locks.

The house is tall and has three floors.
It has a lovely view
Of the canal and of the moors
And other houses too.

There's more room for our pots and pans.
There's more room for our clocks.
There's more room for our Aunts and Grans
At Thirty-two The Locks.

9

The Box Room

The box room is a square shape.
It's cosy, cute and small.
While other rooms have their shape,
The box room is a square shape,
A comfortable-to-wear shape.
I like it best of all.
The box room is a square shape.
It's cosy, cute and small.

What a Mess!

Piles and piles of boxes
Stacked against the wall.
Big and fat and shiny,
Short and thin and tall.

Mountains of them, towers.
They must weigh a ton!
It will take me hours
To open every one.

Most of them are cardboard.
Some of them are wood.
Some of them are metal.
All of them look good.

Mystery and wonder
Lurk inside a few,
With special places under
Their lids that wait for you.

The Suitcase's Song

Why on earth do you want to unpack
When I keep all your clothes in a stack
In my portable box
With a handle and locks
And wheels at the front and the back?

To unpack and desert me is hateful.
I've got room here for more than a crate full.
I have carried your stuff
For, I think, long enough
And the least you can do is be grateful!

Box of Tissues

For every tear
    there is a tissue.

Far or near,
    it's not an issue.

From Windermere
    to Mogadishu,

for every tear
    there is a tissue.

Tiny Box

It fits inside my palm.
I hold it and feel calm.
It keeps me safe from harm.

A tiny box of wood.
And if I've understood
Correctly, something good

Lives in this little place,
This calm and peaceful space:
A doll with a sweet face

Rests on a paper bed.
Listen to the soft tread
Of thoughts inside her head:

The Worry Doll

I live inside a small container.
I'm here to help in times of strife.
If something's bothering your brain, a
Problem in your world and life,

If there's a worry in your head,
A worry that you can't forget,
Then place me underneath your bed,
Leave me there all night and let

Your worrying be taken care of.
I'll do it for you while you snore
And when you wake you'll be aware of
No real worries any more.

Paint Box

I am red.
Bright and bold.
When I shout, "Stop!"
You do as you're told.

Oh, I'm so sad!
That's right: I'm blue.
Oh, woe is me
And boo hoo hoo!

I am yellow:
Light and cheery.
Red can bellow,
Blue's too dreary,
But I'm just the fellow
To warm the weary!

I'm green like trees
and certain seas,
seaweed and peas
but never cheese
(unless it's so old
that it's full of mould!)

Empty Box Blues

Emptiness makes me feel
Miserable, sad.
Put something in me
To stop me going mad.
Your job is to fill me, so

Bring loads of things:
Oranges, bicycles,
Xylophones, strings.

Be kind and fill me with
Lots of weird stuff:
Umbrellas, ballet shoes,
Elephants, fluff —
Should be enough.

Money Box

Give me a shake and hear me jingle.
Money's the thing that makes me tingle.
I'm stinking rich. I'm blinking rich.
Give me some coins to scratch my itch.
I've made a fortune, made a pot.
Look what a lot of cash I've got.
Put some more pennies in my slot.

New, Strange Land

This box is a new, strange land to visit.
What's inside? Try guessing. Is it

hats or
cats or
mats or
bats or

kings or
rings or
strings or
slings or

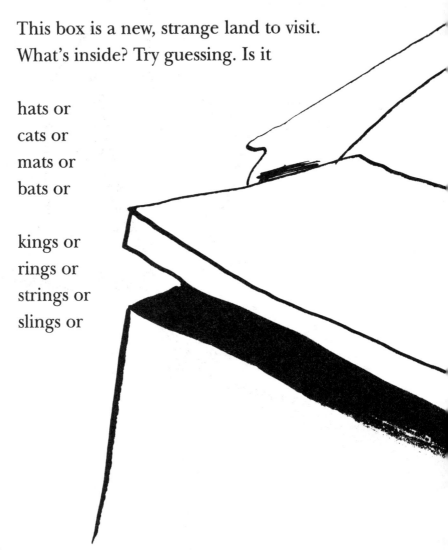

veils or
whales or
scales or
tails or

pigs or
twigs or
is it a jigsaw?

Jigsaw

Piece by piece by piece.
Bit by bit by bit.
House by pond by trees.
Fit by fit by fit.

Sea by sand by beach.
Beach by sea by sand.
Each by each by each.
Air by lake by land.

Fill by fill by fill.
Space by gap by blank.
House by square by mill.
This must be a prank!

Mill by house by square.
Hey! Pass me the box.
What's the picture there?
It's Thirty-two The Locks!

Socks

Four pairs of socks
Leapt out of a box
And they started to do a sock dance

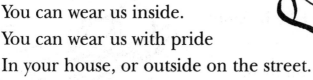

And they sang, "If you put
One of us on your foot
You'll be starting a lifetime's romance.

You can wear us inside.
You can wear us with pride
In your house, or outside on the street.

Feet are our hobby.
Yes, we're the foot lobby,
And this is a song about feet."

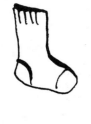

Song of the Square Box

A box should be as high
Or tall as it is wide.
Various rules apply.
The same on every side.

Whether it's full of toys
Or holds a cube of air
Your friend the box enjoys
Being a perfect square.

Boxes cannot be round
Or they will roll away
To where they can't be found
Tomorrow or today.

A box can't be a sphere
That rocks and won't sit still
Or it will disappear,
Go rolling down the hill.

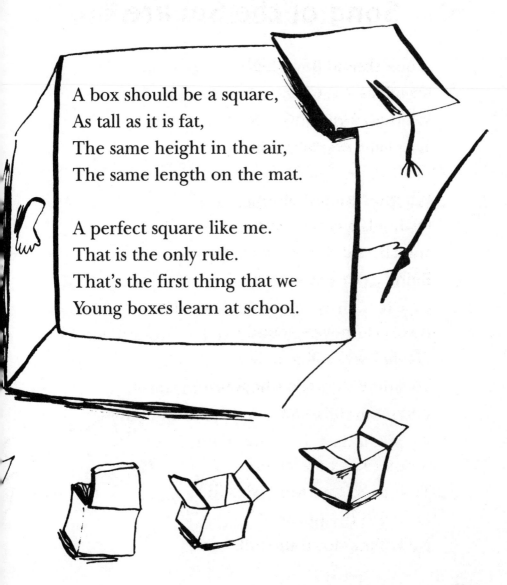

A box should be a square,
As tall as it is fat,
The same height in the air,
The same length on the mat.

A perfect square like me.
That is the only rule.
That's the first thing that we
Young boxes learn at school.

The Round Box Replies

What bilge and nonsense! I have found
A box is just as good when round.
What prejudice! I'm shocked. I'm stunned!
We boxes that are more rotund
Insist upon our full box status.
We have the proper apparatus
Even though mean square boxes hate us.

A box can curve. A box can curl.
Give us a chance. Give us a whirl.
We have round bottoms, we have round lids.
Grown-ups prefer us and so do kids.
We are the shape of moons and suns,
We're the right shape for cakes and buns.
We are, in fact, the chosen ones.

We don't have points that poke and spike.
Corners are something we don't like.
Our forms are gentle, not severe.
Is the world square? No, it's a sphere.
We are the shape of Earth and Mars,
Jupiter, Saturn, all the stars.
Round boxes all deserve hurrahs!

Triangular Boxes
Are Okay Too

I
do not
wish to fuss.
I do not want a wrangle,
But lots of boxes are like us.
Let's have three cheers for the triangle!

Why?

Why do you change when I pass you by,
Box on the wall with your one red eye?

Why do you watch me wherever I go,
Whether I'm moving fast or slow?

Why do you spy on me as I walk,
Box on the wall? Oh, I wish you'd talk!

Why do you sometimes start to ring?
Please will you answer everything?

The Burglar Alarm
Speaks to the Burglar

I'm an alarm.
That is part of my charm.
I stick to the side of the wall.

If you're good, I'll stay calm
But don't dare to do harm
To this house, or you'll hear my shrill call.

So stay at arm's length – that's the length of an arm.
Oh, I am a charming alarming alarm.

I'm small and I'm square.
I can bleep. I can blare,
Make your hair stand on end,
Make you lose all your hair.

I'm the noisiest box
 On the block, on all blocks
In the whole of the town
 So you'd better beware

Because I'm a loud singer,
 A total humdinger
  And just let me ring a
   Policeman or two.
I'm a cracker of crime.
 I've got rhythm and rhyme
  And a lot of free time
   To catch people like you.

So stay at arm's length – that's the length of an arm.
 Oh, I am a charming alarming alarm.

Swimming in the Blue Box

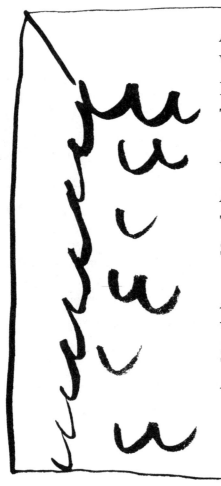

A box of blue
With water in.
It calls to you.
The waves begin.

With water in,
And a lid of light,
The waves begin.
Swim out of sight.

A lid of light,
Wobbly and cool.
Swim out of sight
Around the pool,

Wobbly and cool.
Little blue tiles
Surround the pool
For miles and miles.

Little blue tiles
Cover the floor
For miles and miles
And even more.

Cover the floor
With your bare feet
And even more,
Follow the beat,

With your bare feet
And your swimming cap,
Follow the beat
Of the water's lap.

Your swimming cap
Keeps your head dry.
The waters lap
As you float by.

Keep your head dry
And full of calm
As you float by.
Come to no harm.

Full of calm
And light as a wish,
Come to no harm,
Dream of green fish.

Light as a wish,
They swim in the waves.
Dream of green fish
In watery caves.

Swim in the waves
Like a long dream
Of watery caves
And the pool will seem

Like a long dream,
A bit like sleep.
The pool will seem
Lovely and deep.

A bit like sleep
It calls to you.
Lovely and deep,
A box of blue.

35

The Post-box

I'm always open and I hope
That you'll be passing by
Holding a crisp white envelope.
I'm always open and I hope
You'll visit me. I couldn't cope
Without your post. I'd cry.
I'm always open and I hope
That you'll be passing by.

Your letters are my lunch and tea.
Just post them in my mouth
And you'll be sort of feeding me.
Your letters are my lunch and tea.
And then the postman comes and he
Sends them east, west and south.
Your letters are my lunch and tea.
Just post them in my mouth.

After the postman leaves, I'm sad
With all my letters gone.
So hurry, find a writing pad.
After the postman leaves, I'm sad.
I want more letters than I had
Before, so please – write on!
After the postman leaves, I'm sad
With all my letters gone.

Box of Chocolates

Strawberry, caramel, hazelnut, fudge –
Which one do you prefer?
    You be the judge.
Dark chocolate, white chocolate,
    smooth coffee cream.
Chocolate's the motto, yes, chocolate's
    the theme.

Big chocolates, small chocolates,
    fat chocolates, thin.
Chocolate can't lose. Only chocolate
    can win.
Chocolates are topper and chocolates
    are groovy.
Chocolates could star in a
    chocolatey movie.

Is this a mint, or is this a rum truffle?
Chocolatey chaos, it's chocolate kerfuffle.
This one's an orange cream,
that one is cherry.
How much do I like them?
The answer is very!

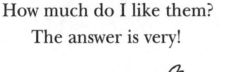

Trouble in the Egg Box

"I was here first
and I will survive,"
one egg said
to the other five.

"I was here next
and I'm better than you,"
said his near neighbour,
egg number two.

"I'm the best looking,"
said the egg by his side,
"too good for cooking.
I will not be fried."

"I'm the most frail.
My life will be spoiled,"
said egg number four,
"if I'm scrambled or boiled."

"I am the strongest,"
said egg number five.
"I can last longest,
so I'll stay alive."

Then egg number six
shouted, "Take me! I'm yours!
I'd rather be omelette
than hear these egg wars."

Microwave

Head's in a spin.
Can't hang about.
The cold goes in
And the hot comes out.

No time to waste.
Time will not wait.
That's why, in haste,
I heat up your plate.

Speed's my device.
Quick is my game.
In goes the ice
And out comes the flame.

Meetings to hold,
Deadlines to meet.
In goes the cold
And out comes the heat.

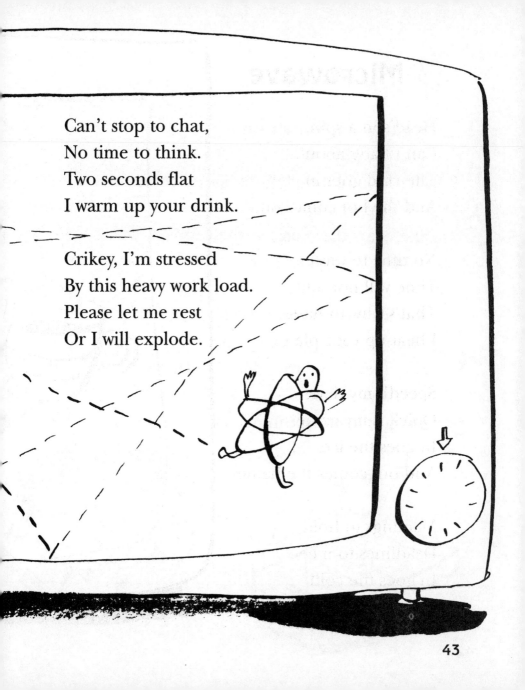

Can't stop to chat,
No time to think.
Two seconds flat
I warm up your drink.

Crikey, I'm stressed
By this heavy work load.
Please let me rest
Or I will explode.

Music Box

See how the ballerina twirls,
The daintiest of all the girls.
Her long blonde hair hangs down in curls
    Tied in a bow.
She hears the music as she whirls
    On her pointed toe.

You lift the lid, she starts to dance
Almost as if she's in a trance.
She doesn't see you, doesn't glance
    At you at all.
She just keeps spinning. There's no chance
    She'll ever fall.

The lid goes up and off she goes.
There is no audience in rows,
No theatre crowds with their Bravos,
    There's only you
And pretty soon the lid will close.
    What will she do?

She'll rest and wait and wait and rest.
Next time you put her to the test
She'll see to it that you're impressed
    With her pirouette.
This little dancing girl's the best
    You've ever met.

Telephone Box

I'm the one box that
can hold a conversation.
Step inside and chat.

The World is a Box

My heart is a box of affection.
My head is a box of ideas.
My room is a box of protection.
My past is a box full of years.

The future's a box full of after.
An egg is a box full of yolk.
My life is a box full of laughter
And the world is a box full of folk.

47

Pick up a Poem
with another Orchard poetry book!

Zoo of Dreams
poems by Adrian Mitchell
pictures by Peter Bailey
ISBN 1 84121 817 0

Come Back to me my Boomerang
poems by John Agard
pictures by Lydia Monks
ISBN 1 84121 748 4

Fluff and other stuff
poems by Tony Mitton
pictures by Philip Hopman
ISBN 1 84121 813 8